I spy

a lizard,

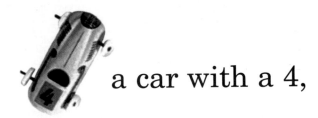 a car with a 4,

a soccer ball,

 and a dinosaur.

I spy

a football jersey,

 a Z,

a lighthouse,

a sun,

and an apple tree.

I spy

 a nickel,

an autumn tree,

peas in a pod,

and a yellow golf tee.

I spy

five leaves,

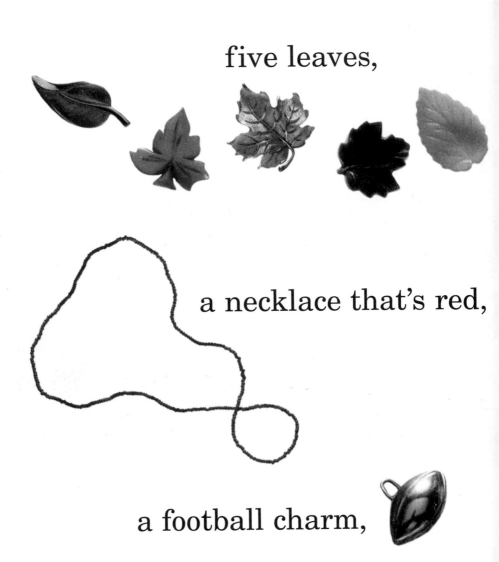

a necklace that's red,

a football charm,

and a shiny wolf's head.

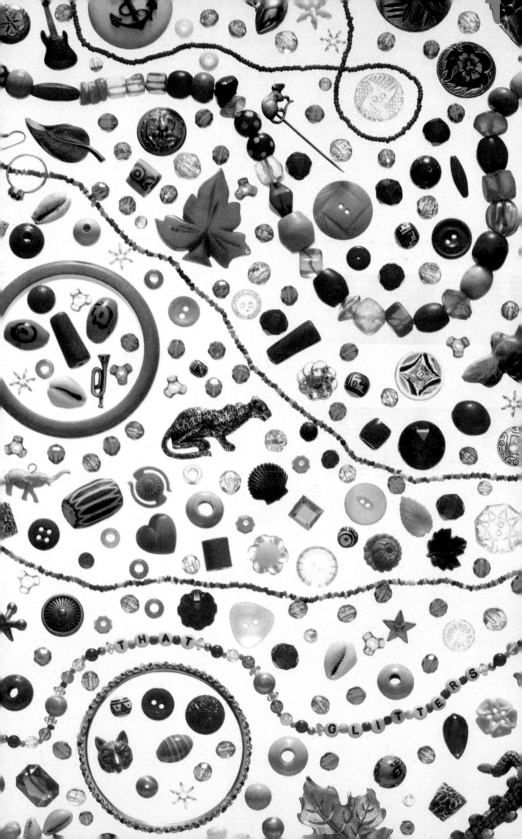

I spy

 a butterfly,

blue striped clothes,

 a THANK you note,

and a little red rose.

I spy two matching words.

 basket of fruit

apple pie

 apple tree

I spy two matching words.

autumn leaf

five leaves

autumn tree

I spy two words that start with the letter N.

blue striped clothes

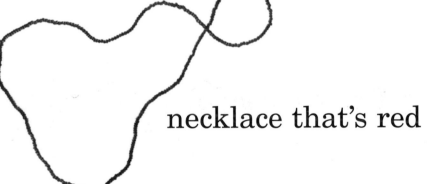

necklace that's red

THANK you note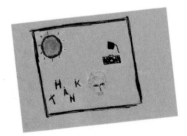

I spy two words that start with the letters CH.

 frog in a chair

football charm

 shiny wolf's head

I spy two words that end with the letter L.

nickel

 musical bear

two fish

I spy two words that end with the letters RD.

 Thanksgiving bird

cap of a jar

 lizard

I spy two words that rhyme.

 dinosaur

truck

 baby duck

I spy two words that rhyme.

 wolf's head

red house

 peas in a pod